I0475868

WHAT EVERYONE SHOULD KNOW ABOUT THE LEGAL LANDSCAPE RELATING TO TESTING

Presented at
ATP Innovations Conference
March 6, 2017

©2017

Regardless of whether an assessment is used for employment, academic, certification, licensure, or credentialing purposes, a range of legal issues can arise. This publication provides an overview of some of the more significant legal issues that might be encountered in the operation of a testing program. It should NOT be viewed as a comprehensive discussion of the topics addressed or as providing legal advice. Seek the assistance of counsel when specific legal issues arise.

Robert A. Burgoyne
Norton Rose Fulbright US LLP
799 9th Street NW, Suite 1000
Washington, DC 20001-4501
robert.burgoyne@nortonrosefulbright.com
(202) 662-4513

Alan J. Thiemann
ATP Counsel
Law Office of Alan J. Thiemann
700 12th Street, NW, Suite 700
Washington, DC 20005
ajthiemann@gmail.com
(202) 904-2467

©2017

CONTENTS

©2017

©2017

OVERVIEW

Like every industry, the testing industry encounters a range of legal issues:

- **Litigation**

  - General litigation (*e.g.*, employment or contract-related litigation)

  - Litigation specific to the nature of the organization (*e.g.*, test security litigation)

- **Regulatory Compliance Issues**

  - Regulations applicable to all similar entities (*e.g.*, ADA regulations)

  - Adjudication by an agency against a specific organization

- **Contracts, Personnel Issues, Etc.**

- **Corporate and Governance Issues**

- **Tax-Related Issues**

This publication focuses on testing-specific litigation and regulatory issues.

TEST-RELATED LITIGATION

A checklist for putting yourself in a position to pursue all possible remedies

√ Test registration/brochure language

It is important that a testing organization develop -- and then implement on a consistent basis -- policies needed to conduct its programs in a manner that protects the integrity of the exam process while respecting the rights of test takers. The policies should address requirements that apply before testing (*e.g.*, prohibiting advance access to secure test content), during testing (*e.g.*, using unauthorized aids or copying from other examinees), and after testing (*e.g.*, participating in "brain dumps" or otherwise disclosing secure content). Testing organizations often use a test taker form or agreement to inform examinees of applicable policies, in addition to publishing policies in exam booklets and on their websites. The critical point here is to ensure that prospective examinees are notified of their rights and obligations as test takers, as well as the potential consequences if they violate those obligations.

√ Capturing the examinee's signature

Having set forth applicable policies, it is equally important for the testing organization to obtain each test taker's acknowledgement of and agreement to be bound by those policies. Courts view the arrangement between a test taker and a testing organization as contractual, with the terms of the contract spelled out in the test-taker agreement and applicable testing policies. Testing organizations should therefore get each examinee's "signature" on language that references the applicable policies and states that the candidate agrees to comply with those polices. Indeed, many organizations obtain a test taker's signature both at the time of registration and again at the testing site. This can be done with an actual signature or an electronic "signature," such as clicking "I agree" on a computer screen before the candidate can proceed to the next page.

 ©2017

√ Proper registration of copyrighted works

Under U.S. law, an organization does not have to register its work to receive copyright protection – this is known as a "common law copyright." However, there are significant legal benefits associated with formal registration, including the right to pursue important remedies under the Copyright Act. It is therefore essential to register all secure exam content and worthwhile to do so even with non-secure content. Registration is required before the owner of the work can bring a copyright infringement lawsuit. If the work is registered within three months of its publication date or before a specific infringement occurs, the copyright owner can recover "statutory" damages (*i.e.*, damages that do not depend on the actual damages suffered by the copyright holder or the profits earned by the infringer). The copyright owner may also be able to recover attorney's fees if its infringement lawsuit is successful.

Two cases of possible interest here:

Reed Elsevier, Inc. v. Muchnick, 559 U.S. 154 (2010) (failure to register a work does not limit the federal court's subject matter jurisdiction over a claim of infringement)

Pacific Stock, Inc. v. Pearson Education, Inc., 2012 WL 93182 (D. Hawaii 2012) (concluding that defendant failed to show that plaintiff had not validly registered its copyright)

√ Contracts with vendors to allocate respective responsibilities

When a test sponsor contracts with another entity to develop or administer an exam, the contract should carefully spell out the parties' respective responsibilities regarding protecting exam content, as well as the remedies available for a breach of the contractual obligations.

√ Cease-and-desist letters

When an organization finds that its copyrighted materials are being infringed (*i.e.*, used without permission and where no other justification exists). a common first line of defense is to send a "cease and desist" letter. By putting the infringer on notice, the owner might prevent further infringements in a relatively cost-effective manner. In addition, the notice puts the copyright owner in a better position to assert that the infringement was willful, if infringement continues after notice is provided. The Copyright Act authorizes courts to award higher statutory damages for willful infringements.

One word of caution. Before sending a cease-and-desist letter, make sure you have taken steps to capture all available evidence of infringement, including not only the content that is believed to be infringing, but also website posts referring, for example, to test prep questions as "actual questions," or other useful material. Infringing parties often take steps to reduce their exposure once they learn that their infringements have been identified. Because of this concern, some testing entities choose not to send a cease-and-desist letter before filing suit, particularly if they plan to file a complaint and seek immediate *ex parte* relief that will allow them to impound suspected infringing content.

√ Take-down notices

For online infringement, a copyright holder should also consider remedies available under the Digital Millennium Copyright Act ("DMCA"). *See* 17 U.S.C. §§ 512, 1201. Under the DMCA, an organization may send a "takedown" notice to the Internet Service Provider ("ISP") that hosts the infringing content, identifying the materials that must be removed (or access to which is to be disabled). In addition, where the copyright owner finds that an infringer reposts its materials (the so-called "whack-a-mole" problem), an organization may be able to subpoena the ISP to obtain the identity of the owner of the infringing website, as a predicate for suing the infringing party.

 ©2017

This procedure was used in the case discussed below:

In re DMCA Subpoena to eBay, Inc., No. 15cv922 (S.D. Cal.), Order dated June 5, 2015 (upholding the subpoena in a non-testing case even when the infringing materials have been taken down under the DMCA, but narrowing the subpoena's scope to information "sufficient to identify the alleged infringer").

NOTE: For a more detailed discussion of steps that can be taken to protect secure exams, *see* ATP Security Committee, "Guidelines for Legal Protection of Assessment Content" (Jan. 2015).

LAWSUITS RELATING TO UNAUTHORIZED USE OF EXAM CONTENT OR TRADEMARKS

Regardless of whether a cease-and-desist letter or DMCA takedown notice is used or has the desired result, litigation is an available remedy for the unauthorized use of exam content (secure or non-secure) or trademarks. Most such litigation involves civil lawsuits filed in the U.S. However, criminal actions are also pursued on occasion in the U.S., and some testing entities have sued in foreign courts to protect their intellectual property.

Illustrative Civil Cases From U.S. Courts

American Board of Internal Medicine v. Mukherjee, 2011 U.S. Dist. LEXIS 8885 (E.D. Pa. 2011) (holding that the court had personal jurisdiction over defendant with respect to ABIM's claim that defendant breached her examinee agreement by disclosing test questions to a test prep company after testing, but lacked personal jurisdiction over defendant with regard to ABIM's copyright and misappropriation claims)

American Board of Internal Medicine v. Von Muller, 2012 U.S. Dist. LEXIS 94436 (E.D. Pa. 2012) (denying post-trial motions of defendant examinee who had purchased "actual ABIM ... exam questions [from a test prep company] for $480 plus her promise to provide actual test questions to [the company] after she took the examination," and affirming the jury's finding that defendant infringed ABIM's copyrights and breached the "Pledge of Honesty" that she had signed by doing a post-exam "brain dump" and sending 50-75 questions to the prep company; ABIM awarded damages and attorneys' fees), *fee award vacated and remanded for recalculation*, 2013 U.S. App. LEXIS 18941 (3d Cir. 2013)

American Registry of Radiologic Technologists v. Bennett, 2013 U.S. Dist. LEXIS 120548 (W.D. Tex. 2013) (entering judgment for ARRT on its claims of copyright infringement, breach of contract, tortious interference, and misappropriation of trade secrets against a test prep company and its owner, where defendants encouraged students to memorize questions from actual exam and send them to the test prep company for distribution to other students)

American Registry of Radiologic Technologists v. Hansen, 2008 U.S. Dist. LEXIS 100442 (C.D. Cal. 2008)(consent judgment entered in ARRT's favor on its copyright, unfair competition, and breach of contract claims against a web-based test prep company and its owner, where owner tested multiple times and also paid students to send in questions they remembered, in violation of their non-disclosure agreement; ARRT awarded injunctive relief and damages of $250,000, with damage award satisfied by transferring all of the defendants' test prep-related assets to ARRT)

 ©2017

Ass'n of American Medical Colleges v. Mikaelian, 571 F. Supp. 144 (E.D. Pa. 1983) (preliminarily enjoining test prep company's unauthorized use of copyrighted MCAT questions), *aff'd mem.*, 734 F.2d 3 (3d Cir. 1984), *subsequent proceeding*, 1986 U.S. Dist. LEXIS 28062 (E.D. Pa. 1986) (holding prep company and its owner in contempt for violating prior injunction, and awarding AAMC damages for the additional infringements)

Ass'n of American Medical Colleges v. Princeton Review, Inc., 332 F. Supp. 2d 11 (D.D.C. 2004) (granting in part AAMC's motion to dismiss counterclaims asserted by a test prep company, and striking certain of the defendant's affirmative defenses)

Chicago Board of Education v. Substance, Inc., 354 F.3d 624 (7th Cir. 2003) (affirming lower court's finding that a teacher infringed the copyrights in high school achievement tests by publishing questions in a newspaper to illustrate his view that they were "bad tests," and rejecting "fair use" defense)

Cisco Technology, Inc. v. Certification Trendz Ltd., 2015 U.S. Dist. LEXIS 83125 (D. Conn. 2015)(granting Cisco's *ex parte* application for a temporary restraining order and temporary impoundment order, based upon Copyright Act and Lanham Act claims, against three web-based companies that sell prep materials for Cisco certification exams under the names TestKing.com, Pass4Sure.com, TestInside, and TestInside.com); *and* 2015 U.S. Dist. LEXIS 83127 (D. Conn. 2015)(granting Cisco's *ex parte* application for a temporary restraining order freezing defendants' financial accounts and assets)

Educational Testing Service v. Katzman, 793 F.2d 533 (3d Cir. 1986) (affirming preliminary injunction against test prep company based on claimed infringement for cloning live items from SAT exams and achievement tests, and rejecting fair use defense), *aff'g* 626 F. Supp. 527 (D.N.J. 1985)

Educational Testing Service v. Simon, 95 F. Supp. 2d 1081 (C.D. Cal. 1999) (judgment entered in favor of ETS on copyright and California state law claims against test prep company for unauthorized use of questions from a teacher licensing exam)

Graduate Management Admission Council v. Raju d/b/a "Gmatplus.Com", 241 F. Supp. 2d 589 (E.D. Va. 2003) (holding that court had personal jurisdiction over individual in India who operated a web-based test preparation service), *later proceeding*, 267 F. Supp. 2d 505 (E.D. Va. 2003) (entering judgment in favor of GMAC on its copyright infringement claims)

Graduate Management Admission Council v. Lei Shi, d/b/a "Scoretop.com," 2007 U.S. Dist. LEXIS 95920 (E.D. Va. 2007) (Magistrate's report recommending that default judgment be entered against operator of web-based test preparation service for infringing GMAC's copyrights in the GMAT, and that GMAC be awarded $7.7 million in damages, attorneys' fees and injunctive relief), *recommendations adopted*, 2008 U.S. Dist. LEXIS 1621 (E.D. Va. 2008)

In re: Charles M. Frye, Debtor, 2008 Bankr. LEXIS 4686 (9th Cir. Bankr. 2008) (affirming award of $6 million for willful copyright infringement and misappropriation of trade secrets where defendant instructed students to reconstruct exam questions, and holding that the damages were not subject to discharge in bankruptcy because they resulted from willful misconduct)

Microsoft Corp. v. Yan, 2010 U.S. Dist. LEXIS 14933 (D. Conn. 2010)(granting Microsoft a preliminary injunction, based on Copyright Act and Lanham Act claims, against multiple defendants who distributed infringing Microsoft certification exam materials by way of various websites, including testinside.com, pass4side.com, certinside.com, and exam4cert.net, enjoining the defendants from distributing such exam materials or transferring their domain names); *and* 2010 U.S. Dist. LEXIS 14934 (D. Conn. 2010)(granting Microsoft a preliminary injunction freezing the defendants' accounts, including their PayPal and Moneybookers accounts)

Nat'l Ass'n of Boards of Pharmacy v. Board of Regents of the Univ. System of Georgia, 633 F.3d 1297 (11th Cir. 2011) (affirming lower court's holding that plaintiff could not recover damages against the state defendants because Congress had not validly abrogated the state's sovereign immunity, where a professor had gathered "actual NAPLEX questions for use in a … review course he was teaching" by "having recent examinees send him questions they remembered;" damage claims against the professor in his individual capacity for infringing the plaintiff's copyrights, misappropriating plaintiff's trade secrets, and breaching a prior settlement agreement were not addressed by the appellate court and remained for resolution on remand)

Nat'l Commission for the Certification of Crane Operators v. Ventula, 2009 U.S. Dist. LEXIS 120921 (D. Haw. 2009)(Magistrate's Report granting plaintiff a default judgment and permanent injunction against an individual who was distributing plaintiff's copyrighted exam materials), *recommendations adopted*, 2010 U.S. Dist. LEXIS 7172 (D. Hawaii 2010)

Nat'l Board of Medical Examiners v. Optima University LLC, 2011 U.S. Dist. LEXIS 143645 (W.D. Tenn. 1989)(holding that test prep company and its owner "directly and contributorily infringed upon the copyrighted USMLE questions of the NBME," and awarding statutory damages of $2.4 million, attorney's fees, and injunctive relief)

Nat'l Conference of Bar Examiners v. Multistate Legal Studies, d/b/a PMBR, 458 F. Supp. 2d 252 (E.D. Pa. 2006) (holding that test prep company infringed NCBE's copyrights in the MBE and awarding NCBE roughly $12 million in damages, attorneys' fees, and injunctive relief)

Nat'l Conference of Bar Examiners v. Saccuzzo, No. 03-CV-0737, 2003 U.S. Dist. LEXIS 28358 (S.D. Cal. 2003) (consent judgment entered in favor of NCBE on its copyright and California state law claims against test preparation company and its owners)

Nat'l Council of Examiners for Engineering and Surveying v. Cameron-Ortiz, 626 F. Supp. 2d 262 (D.P.R. 2009) (judgment entered in favor of NCEES on its copyright and breach-of-contract claims against an examinee caught videotaping exam content while testing)

Illustrative Criminal Cases From U.S. Courts

U.S. v. Hedaithy, 392 F.3d 580 (3d Cir. 2004) (affirming convictions for conspiracy to commit mail fraud, where defendants participated in a scheme to have imposters take the TOEFL exam so that the purported examinees would remain eligible to live in the U.S. under a student visa)

U.S. v. Rodriguez-Torres, 570 F. Supp. 2d 237, *and* 560 F. Supp. 2d 108 (D.P.R. 2008) ("In this case, a total of [110] doctors, were charged in an eighty six count Superseding Indictment for having participated in a scheme to improperly obtain a license to practice medicine in Puerto Rico. Specifically, the … Indictment charges Defendant with … Conspiracy to commit an offense to defraud the United States … and … Mail fraud….") (underlying conduct included altering medical licensing exams taken by prospective licensees).

Illustrative Cases From Courts Outside The U.S.

Graduate Management Admission Council & ETS v. Beijing New Oriental School, Beijing High Court, People's Rep. of China (2005) (affirming lower court finding of copyright infringements)

Graduate Management Admission Council v. STN Academy, Seoul Korea Central District Court (2014) (holding that defendant infringed GMAC's copyrighted GMAT questions)

Agency Proceedings Challenging Domain Names

Educational Testing Service v. TOEFL, Case No. WIPO D2000-0044 (March 16, 2000) (finding that the Respondent engaged in an abusive registration of the domain name "toefl.com" and directing the domain name registrar (Network Solutions) to transfer the domain name to ETS)

LAWSUITS AND AGENCY INVESTIGATIONS INVOLVING THE AMERICANS WITH DISABILITIES ACT (ADA) AND SIMILAR STATE LAWS

Title III ADA provision specifically applicable to private testing entities

"Any person that offers examinations or courses relating to applications, licensing, certifications, or credentialing for secondary or postsecondary education, professional, or trade purposes shall offer such examinations or courses in a place and manner accessible to persons with disabilities or offer alternative arrangements for such individuals." 42 U.S.C. § 12189.

Illustrative Cases

Calif. Dep't of Fair Employment & Housing v. Law School Admission Council, No. 12-cv-01830 (N.D. Cal. May 29, 2014) (Consent Decree resolving alleged violations of ADA and California statute relating to testing accommodations and score annotation policy)

Bibber v. Nat'l Board of Osteopathic Med. Exam'rs, 2016 U.S. Dist. LEXIS 48181 (E.D. Pa. 2016) (individual who scored in the 71st percentile on the GRE and in the "average" range on the reading section of the MCAT without accommodations was not substantially limited compared to most people in reading so as to be disabled under ADA)

©2017

Bach v. Law School Admission Council, 2014 U.S. Dist. LEXIS 124632 (M.D.N.C. 2014) (denying preliminary injunction for examinee who was denied accommodations)

Healy v. Nat'l Board of Osteopathic Med. Exam'rs, 870 F. Supp. 2d 607 (S.D. Ind. 2012) ("Matthew's above-average standardized testing scores, ACT scores, and SAT scores, during which he received no accommodation, . . . stand as testament to his ability to read, learn, think, and concentrate just as well, if not better, than the general population.")

Rumbin v. Ass'n of American Medical Colleges, 803 F. Supp. 2d 83 (D. Conn. 2011) ("[T]he evidence of his past employment requiring substantial visual focus, his ability to paint and read books, and his prior education and test-taking without accommodations, demonstrate that he is not substantially limited in the major life activities of seeing, learning, and reading.")

Jones v. Nat'l Conference of Bar Examiners, 801 F. Supp. 2d 270 (D. Vt. 2011) (granting preliminary injunction requiring NCBE to allow a visually impaired examinee to take a paper-based licensing exam on a laptop computer using screen-reader software, and rejecting NCBE's "undue burden" argument because NCBE had previously provided that accommodation to other examinees and could take adequate steps to protect the exam's security), *appeal dism'd as moot*, 2012 U.S. App. LEXIS 8443 (2d Cir. 2012)

Love v. Law School Admission Council, 513 F. Supp. 2d 206, 228 (E.D. Pa. 2007) ("Given ... Plaintiff's test scores, clinical evaluations, educational history, and his reported ability to function in both academic and professional environments, we are not persuaded that Plaintiff has a disability as defined under the ADA.")

Turner v. Ass'n of American Medical Colleges, 167 Cal. App. 4th 1401 (Cal. App. 2008) (holding that California law does not requires testing accommodations for learning and reading-related disabilities, independent of any obligations imposed under the federal ADA)

Title I ADA provisions relating to testing in employment context

"(a) General rule. - No covered entity shall discriminate against a qualified individual on the basis of disability in regard to job application procedures, the hiring, advancement, or discharge of employees, employee compensation, job training, and other terms, conditions, and privileges of employment.
(b) Construction. - As used in subsection (a) of this section, the term 'discriminate against a qualified individual on the basis of disability' includes ... (6) using qualification standards, employment tests or other selection criteria that screen out or tend to screen out an individual with a disability or a class of individuals with disabilities unless the standard, test or other selection criteria, as used by the covered entity, is shown to be job-related for the position in question and is consistent with business necessity; and (7) failing to select and administer tests concerning employment in the most effective manner to ensure that, when such test is administered to a job applicant or employee who has a disability that impairs sensory, manual, or speaking skills, such test results accurately reflect the skills, aptitude, or whatever other factor of such applicant or employee that such test purports to measure, rather than reflecting the impaired sensory, manual, or speaking skills of such employee or applicant (except where such skills are the factors that the test purports to measure)." 42 U.S.C. § 12112; *see also* Section 504 of the Rehabilitation Act, 29 U.S.C. § 794(a), (d), which prohibits entities that receive federal financial assistance and federal Executive agencies from discriminating against individuals "solely by reason of" their disability, and incorporating by reference the ADA Title I standards for determining violations of Section 504.

©2017

Illustrative Cases

Karraker v. Rent-a-Center, Inc., 411 F.3d 831 (7th Cir. 2005) (use of the MMPI for job promotion purposes held to be an unlawful pre-employment medical exam under Title I of the ADA, because certain questions were designed "at least in part" to reveal mental illness)

Jaramillo v. Professional Examination Services, 544 F. Supp. 2d 126 (D. Conn. 2008) (granting summary judgment for defendant State of Connecticut and its subcontractor PES on a blind examinee's claim that the State violated Section 504 of the Rehabilitation Act by not providing an audiotape version of a licensing exam or the use of a computer with adaptive equipment, in addition to the closed caption television (CCTV), live reader and extended testing time that the State had provided)

EEOC v. Daimler Chrysler Corp., 2006 WL 3360629 (E.D. Mo. 2006) (approving a settlement for 12 applicants with learning disabilities who were denied a reader as an accommodation in taking a written pre-employment test)

NOTE: For an early analysis of the use of psychological tests under the ADA, see D.W. Arnold and A.J. Thiemann, "To Test or Not to Test: The Status of Psychological Testing Under the Americans with Disabilities Act," J. of Business & Psychology, Vol. 6, pp. 503-506 (1992).

LAWSUITS RELATING TO...

...Cancellation of test scores

Murray v. Educational Testing Service, 170 F.3d 514 (5th Cir. 1999) ("ETS's contract with Murray clearly and explicitly reserved to ETS the right to withhold any scores ETS had reason to believe were not valid. The only contractual duty ETS owed to Murray was to investigate the validity of Murray's scores in good faith. ETS fulfilled that duty by allowing Murray to present evidence supporting his scores, informing Murray of his right to seek independent review, and ultimately allowing Murray to retake the test. Several courts ... have recognized the importance of allowing ETS to assure itself of the validity of students' scores through internal review procedures. ETS provides a valuable service to colleges and universities by providing a standardized measure of students' ability.")

Langston v. ACT, 890 F.2d 380 (11th Cir. 1989) (rejecting examinee's claims for breach of contract, emotional distress, libel, slander, and denial of due process, where ACT followed its published policies regarding score investigations and plaintiff had agreed to be bound by those policies: "Under the governing law, the outcome of plaintiff's case does not turn on whether or not plaintiff cheated on his exam, but only on whether or not ACT carried out its contractual obligations in good faith.")

Educational Testing Service v. Hildebrant, 923 A.2d 34 (Md. 2007) (affirming summary judgment for ETS on examinee's breach of contract claim, where ETS followed the procedure in its Bulletin and plaintiff had "signed a certification statement indicating that she agreed to the conditions set forth in the Bulletin")

... Alleged errors in test administration or scoring

Patterson v. Nat'l Board of Medical Examiners, 2016 U.S. Dist. LEXIS 162364 (W.D. Okla. 2016) ("[A] brief power outage occurred while plaintiff was taking the Step 2 CS exam. Because the outage may have affected plaintiff's ability to pass the test, the NBME offered plaintiff the opportunity to retake it with no additional fee, which he accepted. Under the terms of the parties' agreement, set out in the 2013 USMLE Bulletin of Information, plaintiff's exclusive remedy for errors in administering Step examinations was to 'retest at no additional fee or to receive a refund of the examination fee.' As defendant provided plaintiff with the exclusive remedy available under the terms of their agreement, his breach of contract claim fails.")

Ellinghaus v. The College Board, 2016 U.S. Dist. LEXIS 139918 (E.D.N.Y. 2016) (dismissing putative class action claims alleging breach of contract, negligence, unjust enrichment, negligent misrepresentation, and violation of various state consumer protection statutes in connection with a printing error in the written instructions provided to examinees on the SAT and the manner in which The College Board responded to the error)

San Mateo Union High School District v. Educational Testing Service, 2013 U.S. Dist. LEXIS 124733 (N.D. Cal. 2013) (upholding decision by ETS and College Board to cancel scores on an AP exam because of violations of examinee seating policies)

In re Educational Testing Service Praxis Principles of Learning & Teaching: Grades 7-12 Litig., 517 F. Supp. 2d 832 (E.D. La. 2007) (allowing certain claims to proceed in a lawsuit involving claims of negligence and breach of contract brought on behalf of 1,500+ test takers who alleged that their teacher certification exams were incorrectly scored between 2003 and 2004; the parties reached a settlement that included a $ 11.1 million settlement fund)

Russo v. NCS Pearson, Inc., 462 F. Supp. 2d 981 (D. Minn. 2006) (dismissing some claims brought against College Board and Pearson following an error in scoring SAT exams, but allowing other claims to proceed)

…Challenging a testing entity's scoring policies or grading

Baji v. Northeast Regional Board of Dental Examiners, 2001 U.S. App. LEXIS 1825 (6th Cir. 2001) (rejecting examinee's negligence claim that was "based on the idea that NERB failed in its professional duty to provide him with a psychometrically valid exam that accurately measures what it purports to, in this case dental competency," which the court characterized as a "testing malpractice" theory for which plaintiff identified no supporting authority: "Challenges by those who fail professional licensing exams are sometimes made, but they very rarely succeed. In Ohio, a court will not substitute its judgment for that of a professional licensing board as to grades received by an applicant for admission to the practice of a profession, unless evidence shows the examination was 'arbitrarily or capriciously graded.' Even where assessment of performance on an examination is somewhat subjective, the result cannot usually be attacked unless the lack of criteria constitutes 'lack of professional judgment' by examiners.")

Kiprilov v. Nat'l Board of Medical Examiners, 2016 U.S. Dist. LEXIS 162705 (C.D. Cal. 2016) (rejecting all legal claims asserted by an examinee who challenged a policy that the three subcomponents of a licensing exam have to be passed in a single administration in order to achieve an overall passing score)

Walsh v. Massachusetts Board of Bar Examiners, 2002 U.S. Dist. LEXIS 6507 (D. Mass. 2002) (rejecting contract and Constitutional claims by an examinee who challenged a change in the minimum passing score required on an attorney licensing exam)

LAWSUITS AND AGENCY INVESTIGATIONS ALLEGING THAT USE OF A TEST IS DISCRIMINATORY

Tests used as a selection criteria (*i.e.*, employment-related tests)

Under the Civil Rights Act of 1964, it is illegal to discriminate against someone (applicant or employee) because of that person's race, color, religion, sex or national origin. The Age Discrimination in Employment Act prohibits discrimination based on age (40 and over). The use of a test in the employment context can thus result in claims of discrimination under federal law.

In 1978, the Equal Employment Opportunity Commission and several other federal agencies adopted the *Uniform Guidelines on Employee Selection Procedures,* to provide "a uniform set of principles" that apply to the "use of tests and other selection procedures" under federal laws prohibiting discriminatory employment practices. *See* 29 C.F.R. §§ 1607.1.A, 1607.1.B. (This citation is to the *Guidelines* as they appear with the EEOC's regulations; the *Guidelines* also appear with the regulations of other agencies by which they have been adopted, such as the U.S. Department of Labor, 41 C.F.R. Part 60-3). Among other things, the *Guidelines* address when the use of tests will be found to be discriminatory because of an adverse impact on members of a protected subgroup. The *Guidelines* "do not require a [test] user to conduct validity studies of selection procedures where no adverse impact results" from use of a test, but they encourage all test users "to use selection procedures which are valid...." 29 C.F.R. § 1607.1(B).

The *Guidelines* built on a 1971 Supreme Court decision that addressed the "disparate impact" theory of employment discrimination. In *Griggs v Duke Power Co*, 401 U.S. 424 (1971), the Court considered the legality of hiring practices which required that applicants possess a high school diploma and pass a general intelligence test. The Court held that if a test has a disparate impact on protected minority groups, the employer must demonstrate that the test is "reasonably related" to the job for which the test is required to justify use of the test as a selection criteria.

NOTE: The *Uniform Guidelines* can be found at https://www.law.cornell.edu/cfr/text/29/part-1607. A set of "Questions and Answers to Clarify and Provide a Common Interpretation of the *Uniform Guidelines* on Employee Selection Procedures," issued by the agencies that adopted the *Guidelines*, is available at https://www.eeoc.gov/policy/docs/qanda_clarify_procedures.html

An EEOC "Fact Sheet" on Employment Tests and Selection Procedures is available at https://www.eeoc.gov/policy/docs/factemployment_procedures.html

An OFCCP Directive addressing "Investigative procedures when a test is one cause of adverse impact in hiring" is available at https://www.dol.gov/ofccp/regs/compliance/directives/dir267.htm

And a handbook by the Department of Labor titled "Testing and Assessment: An Employer's Guide to Good Practices" (1999) is found at https://wdr.doleta.gov/opr/FULLTEXT/99-testassess.pdf

An unlawful adverse impact can occur when a facially neutral employment tool (*e.g.*, test, interview, criminal background check, educational background, etc.) has a substantially negative impact on members of a protected subgroup. In general, if the selection rate for a protected class of applicants is less than 80% of the selection rate for the group with the highest selection rate, there has been a prima facie showing of adverse impact; this is the so-called "4/5th's rule."

NOTE: A comprehensive paper on Disparate Impact, authored by David Arnold, is available at www.wonderlic.com/disparateimpactwhite paper. A well-documented discussion of emerging trends relating to adverse impact and test validity in paper-and-pencil and computer-based testing is found in the Statement of James L. Outtz, Ph.D., submitted in connection with an EEOC Hearing on

©2017

"Employment Testing and Screening" (May 16, 2007), available at https://www.eeoc.gov/eeoc/meetings/archive/5-16-07/outtz.html

Historically, job analysis has been a foundation of applied measurement for managing and defending HR decisions. When developing a test (or battery) for employee selection, the first step is to conduct a job analysis that identifies the critical aspects/functions of the job. Then, the employer identifies the knowledge, skills, and abilities (KSAs) that are needed to perform those critical job functions. Finally, tests that measure those attributes or characteristics can be selected or developed. This analysis applies to testing used for hiring purposes, as well as testing of current employees for promotion or other purposes.

Although roughly 40 years have passed since the *Uniform Guidelines* were adopted, enforcement agencies (DOJ, EEOC and OFCCP) continue to apply the *Uniform Guidelines* literally, despite significant peer-reviewed research and endorsement of validity generalization by the National Research Council. *See, e.g.,* M. McDaniel *et al.*, "The *Uniform Guidelines* are a Detriment to the Field of Personnel Selection," Industrial and Organizational Psychology, 4/494 (2011). Some federal courts, however, have found in favor of generalizing validity evidence for cognitive ability tests without having to conduct local validation studies with investigation of single-group validity. *See, e.g., Bernard v. Gulf Oil Corp.* 890 F.2d 735 (5th Cir. 1989). J. Sharf, "OPM Bringing the Science of Validity Generalization (VG) to Federal Hiring Reform," SIOP TIP, Vol.8 (July 2011), found at www.siop.org/tip/July11/08Sharf.aspx

Here are a few illustrative cases involving employment tests or other selection criteria:

Ricci v. DeSefano, 557 U.S. 557 (2009) (holding that the City of New Haven violated Title VII of the Civil Rights Act when it refused to certify the results from a pre-employment eligibility test for firefighters because the top scorers were predominantly white and the City feared it would be subject to a disparate impact lawsuit; the Court found that the City's actions amounted to "reverse discrimination" because the City could not demonstrate "a strong basis in evidence that, had it not taken the action, it would have been liable" for using a selection criteria with a disparate impact on minority candidates; "strong basis of evidence" is arguably more stringent than a "business justification").

EEOC v. Kaplan Higher Education Corp. (6th Cir. 2014) (affirming summary judgment in favor of defendant where the EEOC used a "flawed methodology" to prove that credit checks conducted by the employer had an unlawful disparate impact, and noting that "the EEOC sued the defendants for using the same type of background check that the EEOC itself uses")

Bew v. City of Chicago, 252 F.3d 891 (7th Cir. 2001) (rejecting Title VII discrimination claim by police officers who failed a certification exam: "Plaintiffs readily admit and the district court correctly found that the certification exam was job related and content valid. In light of this finding and our holding that the cut-off score was appropriate, it stands to reason that defendants may require probationary police officers to pass the certification exam. In other words, requiring plaintiffs to pass an exam, which, despite its disparate impact, is in all ways permissible under Title VII, comports with the business necessity and job related standards.")

Solo Cup Co. v. Federal Ins. Co., 619 F.2d 1178 (7th Cir. 1980) ("[S]tatistical proofs in disparate impact actions, most particularly those involving employment testing, have become increasingly complex and employers now often retain batteries of experts to validate their selection criteria.")

Kerver v. City & County of Denver, Case No. 11-cv-00256 (D. Colo. 2015) (city admitted that test discriminated against minority applicants in 8 of 21 job classifications, leaving damages to be resolved at trial)

EEOC v. Freeman, 961 F. Supp. 2d 783 (D. Md. 2013) (rejecting claim that criminal background checks conducted by the employer resulted in disparate impact, finding that EEOC's expert analysis was "laughable" and "completely unreliable")

Brazile v. City of Houston, 858 F. Supp. 2d 718 (S.D. Tex. 2012) (discussing the issues of proof in disparate impact case involving employment testing)

U.S. v. City of New York, 635 F. Supp. 2d 77 (E.D.N.Y. 2009) (finding that firefighter pre-employment tests did not actually test the abilities purported to be tested and that the job analysis and test construction were "deficient" because the City used panels of existing firefighters to write items instead of independent test experts; the court subsequently ruled that the City intentionally discriminated against minority applicants and awarded damages, but this decision was overturned on appeal in *U.S. v. City of New York,* 2013 WL 1955782 (2d Cir. 2013))

Robinson v. Ford Motor Co., 2005 U.S. Dist. LEXIS 11673 (S.D. Ohio 2005) (approving settlement of nationwide class-action suit on behalf of minorities rejected for an apprenticeship program based on the results of a cognitive test that measured verbal, numeric and spatial reasoning, where use of the test had been validated in 1991 but less discriminatory procedures were subsequently developed and Ford failed to modify its procedures; settlement included development of a new test by an independent psychologist, but EEOC also challenged that test, leading to a second settlement)

NOTE: For a guide that addresses issues and best practices relating to the use of integrity tests in the employment context, see the ATP's "Model Guidelines for Pre-employment Integrity Testing" (3d ed. March 2010), available at the ATP website book store.

NOTE: State laws might also limit the use of tests for employment purposes. *See, e.g., Soroka v. Dayton Hudson Corp.*, 1 Cal. Rptr. 2d 77 (Cal. App. 1991) (preliminarily enjoining Target's use of a psychological screening test that was challenged as violating privacy protections found in the California Constitution and California statutes that prohibit discrimination, where individual test items referred to religion and sexual orientation).

Tests used for admission to academic institutions or scholarships

Clyburn v. Shields, 2002 U.S. App. LEXIS 5752 (2d Cir. 2002) (affirming dismissal of Title VI and Title IX discrimination claims against a law school, where plaintiffs alleged that use of LSAT scores as an admissions factor disadvantaged African American applicants)

Sharif v. N.Y. State Education Dep't, 709 F. Supp. 345 (S.D.N.Y. 1989) (enjoining defendants from relying exclusively on SAT scores in awarding merit scholarships, where plaintiff had shown a likelihood of prevailing on the merits of her claim that the selection procedure had a disparate impact on women in violation of Title IX of the Civil Rights Act, and reasonable alternative procedures were available that had less of an impact), *class action certified*, 127 F.R.D. 84 (S.D.N.Y. 1989)

Proficiency tests for high school graduation

GI Forum v. Texas Educ. Agency, 87 F. Supp. 2d 667 (W.D. Tex. 2000) (holding that use of the Texas Assessment of Academic Skills exam as a requirement for high school graduation did not unlawfully discriminate against minority students or violate their right to due process)

Tests used for licensure

Singh v. Federation of State Medical Boards, 1997 U.S. Dist. LEXIS 3916 (S.D.N.Y. 1997) (rejecting discrimination claim by an examinee who had been licensed in India, where defendants refused to waive an examination requirement for licensure in the U.S.)

Tests used for certification

Gulino v. Board of Ed., 122 F. Supp. 3d 115 (S.D.N.Y. 2015) ("The question presently before the Court is a familiar one in this case: Does a teacher certification exam, developed by the New York State Education Department…, discriminate against a class of African-American and Latino applicants for teaching positions in the New York City public school system, in violation of Title VII of the Civil Rights Act of 1964? This Court previously answered that question affirmatively regarding two different incarnations of the Liberal Arts and Sciences Test (the 'LAST'), a certification exam no longer in use. The Court must now answer the same question for the LAST's successor: the Academic Literacy Skills Test (the 'ALST'). Plaintiffs contend that, like its predecessors, the ALST discriminates against the members of the class. The Court disagrees. Unlike the LAST, the ALST qualifies as a job related exam under Title VII. In 2010, in conjunction with its application for the United States Department of Education's Race to the Top program, New York State adopted new federal and state pedagogical and curricular standards that redefined the role of teacher. The ALST was derived from those standards, and thus was appropriately designed to ensure that only those applicants who possess the necessary knowledge, skills, and abilities to teach successfully may be hired to do so in New York's public schools. That conclusion relieves New York City of Title VII liability in this case.")

Antitrust lawsuits

Massachusetts School of Law v. American Bar Ass'n, 107 F.3d 1026 (3d Cir. 1997) (rejecting antitrust claim against multiple defendants that was based, in part, on a law school accreditation requirement relating to use of the LSAT exam as an admissions factor)

Papay v. Haselhuhn, 2010 U.S. Dist. LEXIS 112272 (S.D.N.Y. 2010) (dismissing antitrust claim that was based upon "New York State's designation of the [American Registry of Radiologic Technologists] as its sole agent in administering the exam that is used to determine whether a license to practice radiology should be granted to an individual")

RESPONDING TO DISCOVERY REQUESTS OR THIRD-PARTY SUBPOENAS

Testing entities and testing professionals are sometimes asked to provide copies of secure test materials in response to a discovery request or a court or agency subpoena. Any such request should be evaluated in light of copyright law and the ethical obligations of psychologists and other professionals to protect the value of secure tests, whose psychometric integrity depends upon test takers not having prior access to test materials. Often, this means seeking to quash a subpoena or moving for a protective order from the court.

NOTE: Further discussion of this topic is available in an APA Editorial titled, "Test Security: Protecting the Integrity of Tests," *American Psychologist,* Vol. 54, No. 12, p. 1078 (1999) (available at http://www.apa.org/pubs/journals/amp/test.aspx).

LEGISLATION SPECIFICALLY
ADDRESSING TESTING

Federal copyright regulation for "secure tests"

The following types of "works" are eligible to be copyrighted: test items, item banks, test forms, answers, answer sheets (formats and layouts); test materials (*e.g.*, blueprints, frameworks manuals, user guides), graphic designs, scoring algorithms and rubrics, delivery software, including mobile apps. For tests that are "secure" -- that is, "non-marketed" tests on which items are intended to be used multiple times, and for which the integrity of the test results would be compromised if test takers were able to see the items before taking the test -- a unique copyright registration process exists that enables the applicant to avoid the normal requirement that a copy of the work for which protection is sought be filed with the Copyright Office (and thus available to the general public). Secure test copyrights are handled by a meeting with an examiner in the Copyright Office, and the owner does not have to leave behind a copy of the work.

NOTE: The secure test regulations are found at 37 C.F.R. § 202.20(b)(4) and 202.20(c)(2)(vi). For additional information, see Copyright Office Circular 64, "Copyright Registration of Secure Tests" (available at **www.copyright.gov/circs/circ64.pdf).** Similar regulations are available for registration of software copyrights that include trade secrets (*e.g.*, scoring software): see Copyright Office Circular 61, "Copyright Registration for Computer Programs" (available at **www.copyright.gov/circs/circ61.pdf**) As of the date on which this booklet was prepared, the Register of Copyrights was in the process of revising its procedures for examining secure tests for copyright registrations, anticipated to go into effect in March or April 2017, which may particularly impact the registration of test item banks. The ATP challenged these procedures because they were being adopted without any input from the testing industry and without required notice and public comment under the Administrative Procedure Act, 5 U.S.C., §553.

State "truth-in-testing" laws

In an effort to protect examinee rights, two states passed laws in the late 1970's that impose various disclosure and reporting obligations on entities that administer certain types of standardized tests. Often referred to as "truth-in-testing" laws, these laws ostensibly open up the testing process, make it more transparent in providing equal opportunities to all test takers, and make test publishers "more accountable." The notion has received occasional attention in other states, but without any comparable laws being enacted. Likewise, national legislation has not been seriously considered.

New York

Effective as of January 1, 1980, New York's truth-in-testing law requires certain entities that develop, sponsor or administer any test that is "used in the process of selection for post-secondary or professional school admissions" to disclose test items after an exam has been administered, make technical studies publicly available along with other test-related information, and offer test takers the right to obtain, along with their scores, copies of the test, their answer sheet, and the test key. The statute also restricts disclosure of test scores by a test agency, and affords certain "due process" rights to examinees "whose scores are being questioned for suspected inauthenticity or irregularity in test administration." *See generally* N.Y. Ed. Law §§ 340 *et seq.* The statute's disclosure provisions have been successfully challenged in court:

College Entrance Examination Board v. Pataki, 889 F. Supp. 554 (N.D.N.Y. 1995) (granting a preliminary injunction against enforcement of New York's truth-in-testing law based on the plaintiffs' likelihood of success in showing that the state law was preempted by the federal Copyright Act, but narrowing the injunction to maintain the disclosures that were voluntarily being made), *on reconsideration,* 893 F. Supp. 152 (N.D.N.Y. 1995) (modifying injunction to clarify required partial disclosures)

Ass'n of American Medical Colleges v. Carey, 728 F. Supp. 873 (N.D.N.Y. 1990) (holding that the federal Copyright Act preempted parts of New York's truth-in-testing law), *rev'd*, 928 F.2d 519 (2d Cir. 1991) (holding that factual disputes made summary judgment improper, and remanding for further proceedings; parties eventually settled, with New York amending the statute to limit the disclosures required for the MCAT exam)

California

California passed its version of "truth in testing" legislation earlier than New York, in 1978. *See* Cal. Ed. Code §§ 99150 *et seq*. Applicable to any test that "is used for the purposes of admission to, or class placement in, postsecondary educational institutions or their programs, or any test used for preliminary preparation for those tests," *id*. at § 99151(c), the California statute is not as stringent as the New York law. In particular, it does not require that "secure" tests be filed with the state or returned to students. Instead, as currently amended, it requires that test sponsors file annually with the state's Postsecondary Education Commission copies of any tests that were disclosed in the prior year by the test sponsor, along with certain financial and administration information and technical data on the psychometric properties of the test. It also requires the test sponsor to provide to test takers information on the purposes and scoring of the test and interpretation of scores, as well as "an opportunity to examine operational test questions and answers under closely monitored conditions." *Id*. at 99157(a). In addition, the statute imposes certain requirements on the test sponsor relative to its handling of allegations of "collusion, cheating or irregularity," *id*. at § 99159, and to examinee identification requirements.

NOTE: Further information regarding truth-in-testing laws is available in the following sources: (1) "Truth in Testing Act of 1979: The Educational Testing Act of 1979," Hearings Before the Subcommittee on Elementary, Secondary, and Vocational Education, Committee on Education and Labor, U.S. House of Representatives, 96th Congress (Washington, D.C., U.S. GPO,

1980); (2) "The Educational Testing Act of 1981," Joint Hearings Before the Subcommittee on Postsecondary Education, Committee on Education and Labor, U.S. House of Representatives, 97th Congress (Washington, D.C., U.S. GPO1982); (3) Education Commission of the States, *Searching for the Truth About "Truth in Testing" Legislation,* Report No. 132 (Denver 1980).

State Laws Addressing Efforts To Compromise Exam Security

Some states have laws that make it unlawful to subvert certain types of exams. For example, California has enacted the following law: "It is a misdemeanor for any person to engage in any conduct which subverts or attempts to subvert any licensing examination or the administration of an examination, including, but not limited to: (a) Conduct which violates the security of the examination materials; removing from the examination room any examination materials without authorization; the unauthorized reproduction by any means of any portion of the actual licensing examination; aiding by any means the unauthorized reproduction of any portion of the actual licensing examination; paying or using professional or paid examination-takers for the purpose of reconstructing any portion of the licensing examination; obtaining examination questions or other examination material, except by specific authorization either before, during, or after an examination; or using or purporting to use any examination questions or materials which were improperly removed or taken from any examination for the purpose of instructing or preparing any applicant for examination; or selling, distributing, buying, receiving, or having unauthorized possession of any portion of a future, current, or previously administered licensing examination; (b) Communicating with any other examinee during the administration of a licensing examination; copying answers from

©2017

another examinee or permitting one's answers to be copied by another examinee; having in one's possession during the administration of the licensing examination any books, equipment, notes, written or printed materials, or data of any kind, other than the examination materials distributed, or otherwise authorized to be in one's possession during the examination; or impersonating any examinee or having an impersonator take the licensing examination on one's behalf." Cal. Bus. & Prof. Code § 123. California also has a law that allows a civil lawsuit to be filed to recover damages based upon the violation of another state law. See Cal. Bus. & Prof. Code § 17200. As a result, a test organization can sue for damages based upon a violation of the California law that prohibits exam subversion. *See, e.g., Nat'l Conference of Bar Examiners v. Multistate Legal Studies*, 413 F. Supp. 2d 485, 488-89 (E.D. Pa. 2005) (applying the two California laws in a suit involving a test prep company's efforts to compromise the Multistate Bar Examination).

State laws that require use of an exam for licensure or certification purposes

All states have laws that require professionals to pass a proficiency examination as part of the process for becoming licensed or certified to pursue a particular profession. In many instances, these statutes or regulations reference a specific examination (*e.g.*, the United States Medical Licensing Examination for prospective physicians, the Multistate Bar Examination for prospective lawyers, and the Academic Literacy Skills Test for teacher certification).

PRIVACY AND DATA PROTECTION LAWS

EU Privacy Laws

The European Union (EU) took the lead in enacting broad privacy protections for personal information, and the U.S. has subsequently worked with the EU to harmonize how to apply privacy laws across the EU and the U.S. The EU-US Privacy Shield is the recent framework of robust, transparent, and enforceable protections for the personal data of EU citizens (28 countries, although that will change if and when the UK leaves the EU), predicated on privacy law changes in the EU coming in May 2018, when the General Data Protection Regulation ("GDPR") takes effect. Testing organizations are likely to be impacted. For example, many U.S. test publishers register EU citizens to take tests, handle credit card information from those EU citizens, transfer EU citizen data back to the U.S. for processing (*e.g.*, scoring tests), store test data or personal data in the US, or pass data along to third parties in the U.S. (*e.g.*, test center vendors, scoring vendors). Furthermore, ATP members in the U.S. whose tests are used for employment purposes are likely covered because test results for EU citizens may be considered "HR data" under the Privacy Shield, which carries with it additional requirements.

NOTE: A testing organization that performs any of the above actions should review the specific elements of the Privacy Shield and carefully consider whether to register with the U.S. Department of Commerce ("DOC"). *See* https://www.privacyshield.gov/article?id=How-to-Join-Privacy-Shield-part-1 In December 2016, the ATP published a "Checklist for EU-US Privacy Shield Registration," including a sample Privacy Policy, that is available through the ATP Bookstore on the ATP website.

Canadian Privacy Laws

The Personal Information Protection and Electronic Documents Act ("PIPEDA") lays out the rules governing private-sector organizations in Canada regarding how they collect, use or disclose personal information in the course of commercial activities. PIPEDA does not apply if an organization is doing business wholly within a province that has its own law that has been deemed to be "substantially similar" to PIPEDA (*i.e.*, Alberta, British Columbia, Quebec). There can be conflicts between US and Canadian laws that create practical compliance problems for US organizations. Compliance with PIPEDA is overseen by the Office of the Privacy Commissioner of Canada.

U.S. Privacy Laws Enforcement

Generally, the Federal Trade Commission ("FTC") has jurisdiction over advertising and marketing activities of U.S. businesses, including the information they provide to consumers relative to their privacy policies (*e.g.*, how the business protects information collected on its website and/or other online activities). Thus, even when a testing organization is handling only personal data of US residents, it needs to pay careful attention to how it is protecting personally-identifiable information of its customers, including test takers. Most often these protections are posted on a test sponsor's website and/or set forth in a test taker agreement or form, so that all test takers are told what the organization does to protect their information.

Children's Online Privacy

If an organization operates a website or online service (including mobile apps) directed at at children under 13 years of age, it has to comply with the FTC's rules implementing the Children's Online Privacy and Protection Act ("COPPA"). The rules also apply to websites or online services that have actual knowledge that they are collecting personal information directly from users of another website or online service that is directed to children. Most importantly, the rules require the operator to give notice to parents and obtain verifiable parental consent before collecting personal information online from children.

NOTE: For additional information on the COPPA rules, see https://www.ftc.gov/tips-advice/business-center/guidance/complying-coppa-frequently-asked-questions

Card Payment Data

A specific subset of data protection laws in the US involves the capture, transmission, processing and storage of cardholder financial information (*e.g.* credit or debit cards used to pay for test registrations). Usually the test sponsor as the "merchant" (or a third party vendor acting on its behalf) has the responsibility to protect that financial information by conforming to extensive security procedures adopted by the payment card industry ("PCI") (*e.g.*, Visa, MasterCard, American Express, Discover). The PCI Data Security Specifications ("PCI-DSS") are aimed at preventing data breaches (*e.g.*, Target) where cardholder information is stolen. Almost every state has a Breach Notification law that requires a merchant to notify every cardholder as soon it discovers there has been a data breach; because there is no uniform federal law, a test organization must comply with the state laws in every state for which it has cardholder data –for a national testing program, that probably means all 50 states. Not only is breach notification costly, but the merchant is subject to fines from the card networks (*e.g.*, Visa, MasterCard) and can also be exposed to litigation brought by card issuers to cover the cost of replacing cards for which data was stolen and/or paying for credit-monitoring services.

Privacy of education records

For testing organizations engaged in educational testing, other privacy laws come into play. Chief among these is the Family Educational Rights and Privacy Act ("FERPA"). FERPA protects the privacy of student education records, including test-related information. The law applies to a state education agency (SEA), a local educational agency (LEA), and a school that receives funds under an applicable program of the U.S. Department of Education.

NOTE: The FERPA statute is found at 20 U.S.C. § 1232g; the Department of Education implementing regulations are found at 34 C.F.R. Part 99. The Department of Education has issued a document titled, *Protecting Student Privacy While Using Online Educational Services: Requirements and Best Practices* (2014); it has also issued Model Terms of Service (2015), which set forth all of the terms to which a user of an online service is agreeing when the user "clicks" to accept the service or to access it for the first time. This guidance ties FERPA together with COPPA in an educational testing environment. The Department of Education guidance can be found at http:/ptac.ed.gov

Numerous states also have laws that address the privacy of student education records. For example, a West Virginia student privacy law has served as a model for similar laws in a number of states, as noted in an article that discusses how a state education department should deal with districts and vendors. *See* http://www.nasbe.org/wp-content/uploads/Vance_WV-final.pdf

As a second example, California's Student Online Personal Information Protection Act ("SOPIPA") protects the use of student educational data by third-party vendors. SOPIPA prohibits online education service operators from selling student data, using student data to target advertising, or "amassing a profile" on students for non-educational purposes.

State "open records" laws

On the other side of test-related privacy, many states have laws
that protect testing entities by protecting the confidentiality of
secure test items that will be used again in the future. *See, e.g.,*
N.Y. Public Officers Law § 87(2)(h) (exempting from N.Y.'s
Freedom of Information Law "examination questions or answers
which are requested prior to the final administration of such
questions."). The interplay between these statutes and state
"open records" laws requiring state governmental records to be
made available to the public has been considered in various
court cases, including:

Fla. Dep't of Education v. Cooper, 858 So.2d 384 (Fla. App.
2003) (holding that the statewide assessment (FCAT test booklet
and items) was not a "student record" subject to release at the
request of a parent, and that access was permitted only to test
scores and not the test itself) (ATP filed an *Amicus* brief in this
case (see discussion of *Amicus Curiae* briefs below)

Phoenix Newspapers Inc. v. Keegan, 35 P.3d 105 (Ariz. App.
2001) (newspaper sued to compel disclosure of test items from a
statewide assessment (AIMS), after rejecting Department of
Education's offer to provide access to items but now allow
copying; trial court ordered the release of all items under the
state's Public Records law, except for "anchor items" owned by
CTB, the test publisher, and the court of appeals affirmed)
(ATP filed an *Amicus* brief in this case in the trial court).

State of Ohio ex rel. Rea v. Ohio Dep't of Education, 692 N.E.2d
596 (Ohio 1998) (Ohio Supreme Court ordered disclosure, under
the state's open Public Records law, of the questions from a high
school proficiency test that were developed and owned by Ohio
State University, but held that WorkKeys questions developed
and owned by ACT and included in the state proficiency test
were not subject to disclosure)

PARTICIPATION IN COURT CASES AS
AMICUS CURIAE

Non-parties to a lawsuit are sometimes permitted to file briefs in a case as "*amicus curiae*," which means "friend of the court." Such briefs often focus less on the legal issues presented (which have presumably been adequately addressed by the parties), and more on the broader implications a case might have. Testing-related organizations have filed numerous *amicus* briefs to address issues that are important to the assessment and measurement community and users of test results. In addition to the cases noted above (and others) in which ATP submitted *amicus* briefs, see, for example:

Detroit Edison Inc. v. NLRB, 440 U.S. 301 (1979) (*amicus* briefs filed by the APA, the American Society for Personnel Administration, and the Chamber of Commerce urging the US Supreme Court to protect secure employment tests; the Court agreed that the tests were entitled to reasonable non-disclosure protections: "The Board ... having identified no justification for a remedy granting such scant protection to the Company's undisputed and important interests in test secrecy, we hold that the Board abused its discretion in ordering the Company to turn over the test battery and answer sheets directly to the Unions.")

EEOC v. Kronos Inc., 694 F.3d 351 (3d Cir. 2012), *and* 620 F.3d 287 (3d Cir. 2010) (*amicus* brief filed on behalf of numerous business groups urging the court to protect the integrity of questions used by an employer on employment-related tests by requiring the EEOC to treat any exam content that the EEOC subpoenas from a third-party test developer as confidential)

 ©2017

PROFESSIONAL STANDARDS

Courts often rely on professional standards and professional guidelines in resolving test-related cases: for example:

Hall v. Florida, 134 S. Ct. 1986 (2014) (relying in part upon the DSM-5 in holding that a Florida statute that used an IQ score cutoff of 70 to identify whether a criminal defendant in a capital case had an intellectual disability was unconstitutional)

Griggs v. Duke Power Co., 401 U.S. 424 (1971) (referencing the *Standards for Educational and Psychological Testing*)

LaBar v. McDonald, 2011 U.S. Dist. LEXIS 127897 (E.D. Pa. 2011) (referencing the *Standards for Educational and Psychological Testing*)

Examples of such standards

• *Standards for Educational and Psychological Testing* (2014 ed.) (AERA, APA & NCME)

• *Principles for the Validation and Use of Personnel Selection Procedures* (4th ed. 2003) (Society for Industrial and Organizational Psychology) (5th ed. under review and scheduled to be released in 2018)

• Diagnostic and Statistical Manual of Mental Disorders (5th ed. 2013) (DSM-5) (APA)

• *Code of Fair Testing Practices in Education* (1988) (Joint Committee on Testing Practices)

• *Code of Professional Responsibilities in Educational Measurement* (1995) (NCME)

• *Operational Best Practices in Large Scale Statewide Assessment Programs* (2d ed. 2013) (ATP and Council of Chief State School Officers)

• *ITC Guidelines on Quality Control in Scoring, Test Analysis, and Reporting of Test Scores* (2013) (International Test Commission)

• *ITC Guidelines on Test Use* (2013) (International Test Commission)

TESTING PROFESSIONALS SERVING AS NON-TESTIFYING CONSULTANTS OR EXPERT WITNESSES

As one might guess after reviewing the large number of court cases referenced above, testing professionals are often called upon to serve as consultants or testifying witnesses in test-related litigation. If testifying, the professional might be doing so as a fact witness who happens to also be an expert (*i.e.*, someone who was involved in the events underlying the lawsuit), or as an expert witness with no prior involvement with the parties or the dispute.

In connection with their involvement in such litigation, testing professionals are often asked to disclose sensitive personal information about an individual to whom assessments were administered, or confidential test materials. The information is being disclosed to lawyers and other individuals who may not be ethically or legally obligated to keep these materials confidential, and the information might be admitted into evidence as part of the public record.

In addition to considering possible legal restrictions on the disclosure of such information, such as those imposed under the Health Insurance Portability and Accountability Act (HIPAA), testing professionals from whom such information is requested should consider carefully whether ethical obligations or other constraints exist with respect to providing the requested information. If disclosure of secure test content is requested, the best practice is for the professional to request (through counsel) that a confidentiality agreement be entered into by the parties and a protective order be entered by the court that prohibits parties from making copies or publicly disclosing test content, requires that the materials be returned to the professional at the close of litigation, and seals the record if test questions or answers are admitted as part of the public record.

NOTE: For further discussion on this topic, see British Psychological Society, "Psychologists as Expert Witnesses: Guidelines and Procedure" (4th ed. April 2015), available at http://www.bps.org.uk/system/files/Public%20files/Policy/inf129_april_2015_web.pdf ; T. Gutheil, M.D., "The Psychiatrist as Expert Witness" (2d ed. 2009), available at https://www.appi.org/Psychiatrist_as_Expert_Witness_Second_Edition; J. Wiesen, "Tips for Serving as an Expert Witness," IPAC Conference 2010, available at annex.ipacweb.org/library/conf/10/wiesen.pdf

MISCELLANEOUS RESOURCE MATERIALS

• *Defending Standardized Testing* (2005) (edited by Richard Phelps)

• Briefing for the U.S. Secretary of Education, *Test Security Leading Practices/K-12 Education: States' Test Security Policies and Procedures Varied,* GAO Report No. GAO-13-495R (May 16, 2013)

NOTE: This GAO Report was heavily influenced by the ATP/CCSSO "Operational Best Practices in Large Scale Statewide Assessment Programs" (released in 2010 & updated in 2013)

• Plake, Barbara S. and Jones, Patrick, *The Responsibilities of Test Sponsors, Test Developers, Test Administrators, and Test Takers in Ensuring Fair Testing Practices,* Vol. 4, Issue 1, ATP's Journal of Applied Testing Technology (2002)